moving into the future

buses

An Action Plan for Buses in Scotland

Scottish Executive, Edinburgh 2006

ISBN: 0-7559-5249-9

This document is available on the Scottish Executive website:
www.scotland.gov.uk

Produced for the Scottish Executive by Astron B48680 12/06

Published by the Scottish Executive, December 2006

Further copies are available from
Blackwell's Bookshop
53 South Bridge
Edinburgh
EH1 1YS

Telephone orders and enquiries
0131 622 8283 or 0131 622 8258

Fax orders
0131 557 8149

Email orders
business.edinburgh@blackwell.co.uk

100% of this document is printed on recycled paper and is 100% recyclable

Contents

Foreword by Transport Minister

I want to see modern, reliable, safe and integrated bus services operating throughout Scotland, delivered by public and private partners working well together. Bus services are the principal form of public transport in Scotland. They have huge potential to address each of the key strategic outcomes in the National Transport Strategy – improving journey times and connections; reducing emissions; and improving quality and accessibility and tackling affordability.

Bus operators up and down the country provide high quality services using modern vehicles and well-trained and motivated drivers. Some services are of lower quality. Scotland's growing transport success requires even more commitment to the millions of passengers who use buses day and daily. I want to see all bus operators raise their standards to those of the best, using modern, efficient, low-emission vehicles. I want to see reliable, punctual services, integrating with trains, trams and ferries and encouraging healthy lifestyle choices such as walking and cycling. I want to see local government invest in the high quality road and off-road infrastructure which a modern bus industry needs. Passengers deserve nothing less, no matter where in Scotland they use the bus.

The key stakeholders in the industry – passengers, the Scottish government, national organisations and offices, local government and bus operators – must work closely together in real partnership. We need drive and innovation to improve and develop services for the benefit of current and new bus passengers. This Action Plan therefore is about a better deal for passengers by delivering quality, affordable bus services.

The actions in this Plan will improve the bus experience for passengers and are the starting point for a major drive on buses now and over the next few years. There is great scope for us all to up our game – to plan better, to invest in success, to develop services and to squeeze poor quality out of the system. I commend this Action Plan as the catalyst to make our bus services world class.

Tavish Scott MSP
Transport Minister

DAY TICKET
£2·30
Gorgie
Princes Street
Newington
3
Clovenstone
713
Lothian
Club Class
SN55 BKV

Chapter 1

Introduction, Strategic Direction of Bus Action Plan and Summary of Issues for Buses in Scotland

Introduction

1.1 Buses provide the sustainable mass public transport necessary to support economic growth and accessibility. They are uniquely placed to provide the essential links needed throughout Scotland to enable us all to get to work and to access shops, schools and health services. They are the principal, most frequently used and most widely available mode of public transport. At 84-87%, satisfaction levels are high among bus users across Scotland as a whole.

1.2. Buses are best at providing:

- flexible services, which can be developed and introduced very quickly where demand is identified;
- mass transport in an urban setting, moving large numbers of people - currently around 480 million passenger journeys a year – and thereby reducing the amount of congestion on Scotland's roads and the impact on the environment of emissions;
- accessibility - for many rural, particularly remote rural, areas they provide the only practical alternative to car use.

1.3 Buses in Scotland operate largely in a de-regulated market with the private sector providing the majority of services, backed up by a public sector contribution to the bus and road infrastructure. The Scottish government currently supports buses in Scotland through a range of funding mechanisms (see Chapter 3). There is scope to develop the bus network yet further and improve the standard of service for the millions of people who use the bus. To examine that, the Scottish Executive undertook a Bus Policy Overview in May-June this year which involved interviews with

key stakeholders, Bus User Quality Audits of local bus services, analysis of correspondence from the public and MSPs, and a literature and statistical review conducted by consultants, MVA Consultancy.

1.4. Our vision is for Scotland to have a comprehensive bus network where sustainable bus services are delivered to a high quality, and which move people efficiently to promote economic growth and social inclusion and to reduce congestion. Achieving this vision supports the 3 strategic outcomes of the National Transport Strategy (NTS):

- to improve journey times and connections;
- to reduce emissions; and
- to improve quality and accessibility and tackle affordability.

1.5. *Moving into the Future: an Action Plan for Buses in Scotland* has the potential to make a significant contribution environmentally – in reducing both congestion and emissions – and to the health of Scotland's cities and rural communities by promoting greater accessibility. It will assist disadvantaged people and communities to share in the benefits of economic growth and help Scotland reduce its global environmental and climate impact through sustainable development.

1.6. In turn, the Bus Action Plan helps to deliver the key objectives in the *Framework for Economic Development in Scotland*, *Scotland's Sustainable Development Strategy*, *Scotland's Climate Change Programme* and the *Air Quality Strategy*.

The Bus Regime

The essence of the current bus regime is partnership, backed up by the possibility of franchised services should transport authorities consider it necessary: bus operators seek out market opportunities and drive down costs; local government is responsible for the infrastructure which buses use and for supporting socially necessary services; central government (Westminster) operates the licensing regime; and central government (Holyrood) sets the policy framework and provides resources through various funding mechanisms.

Strategic Direction of Bus Action Plan

1.7 As mentioned, a substantial investment is made by the Scottish government in the bus industry. The Action Plan seeks to establish a higher return on that investment, driving up quality for the benefit of bus users. The Action Plan recognises that there are potentially large additional benefits from building on the strengths that already exist and achieving a step change in bus usage, particularly modal shift from car to bus. It seeks to be alive to the different requirements of different parts of Scotland. The Bus Policy Overview made it clear that while many of the fundamental challenges for the bus industry are the same across Scotland, in important respects there are also unique circumstances in different parts of the country.

1.8 **The Bus Policy Overview concluded that a step change is required in bus service provision and infrastructure if bus services are to meet the needs of current bus users and attract passengers from the car, and that action is required to strengthen a range of policy and financial tools to help shift the quality of provision upwards across the industry. As is made clear in this Chapter, and explicitly in the Actions set out in Chapter 2, that means:**

More effective transport planning, including:

- better planning and co-ordination among transport authorities.

Development of the bus industry, including:

- closer alignment between central government financing and quality on the ground;
- strengthening Quality Partnerships so that they can cover more readily issues such as the frequency and punctuality of services;

Summary of Issues from the Bus Policy Overview

General

Overall, levels of passenger satisfaction among bus users are high (87%) across Scotland as a whole. This reflects the fact that many bus operators provide high quality services which meet their passengers' needs and many transport authorities provide the infrastructural support which bus operators need.

Growth in passenger numbers in recent years has been supported largely by growth in concessionary bus travel.

The decline in passenger numbers since the 1970s has been mirrored by growth in numbers of licensed motor vehicles as car usage increases.

Failure to achieve a step change improvement could result in a decline in some bus networks and gridlock in cities.

Effective Transport Planning

A step change is required in transport planning, partnership working and the policy framework to provide a strong contribution to the economy and communities and to achieve the broader transport aims of modal shift, reduced congestion and environmental impact.

- simplifying the process to enable franchising (i.e. a Quality Contract) where that is seen to be an option by transport authorities.

More rigorous implementation of the regulatory regime, including:

- changes to the regime so that performance problems are addressed quickly and decisively.

Summary of Issues for Buses in Scotland

1.9 The Bus Policy Overview found many examples of excellent bus provision in Scotland, backed up by high levels of overall satisfaction. There has been growth in bus patronage in 6 of the last 7 years, which reverses the longer term decline in bus usage, though the upward trend is influenced by growth in concessionary travel. The regional dimension is highlighted at the end of this Chapter. In broad terms, there are strong examples of partnership in many parts of Scotland, but there are areas – notably in the West of Scotland – where the quality of service is poor and the service in the evenings and on Sundays is restricted. In addition, in parts of rural Scotland, bus services are too thin to provide the service which people seek.

Development of the Bus Industry

Typical concerns relate to personal safety/security, late running, overcrowding and congestion which indicate that improvements in compliance and partnership are needed.

Significant concerns remain about the provision of rural services, the overall quality of bus services in parts of the West of Scotland, and whether enough emphasis is given to bus passenger priority within traffic management planning.

The Scottish government needs to continue to prioritise funding and to provide a supportive policy framework to sustain rural and urban services and the essential partnership working needed to achieve viable and sustainable bus networks.

Local government needs to make a significant commitment to partnership working including consideration of statutory quality measures to develop necessary infrastructure and to support viable bus networks throughout Scotland.

Effective Implementation of Regulatory Regime

The Traffic Commissioner and the Vehicle and Operator Services Agency (VOSA) have key roles to play in achieving consistent levels of compliance and reliability of services.

Effective Transport Planning

1.10 To achieve increased use of public transport and modal shift, improved air quality, and to address issues such as reductions in congestion, requires effective transport planning at local, regional and national levels in a close partnership of all key stakeholders. There is evidence across the UK of good practice (see box on Edinburgh and York) and how to improve bus patronage levels which can be used to drive up the quality of bus services throughout Scotland.

1.11 In planning improvements to bus services, infrastructure measures on local and trunk roads are key factors. These include on-road demand management measures (bus passenger priority measures, bus lanes on key arterial corridors, park and ride, traffic management systems and Bus Rapid Transit on segregated sections of roadway). The evidence shows that effective partnership working requires transport authorities as their part of the partnership to introduce appropriate infrastructure measures to improve bus passenger journey times. This is the case in relation to the introduction of any quality measure – voluntary or statutory Quality Partnerships, Punctuality Improvement Partnerships or Quality Contracts. The review of the Scottish government bus subsidy regime (Action 4 in Chapter 2) will consider whether financial incentives should be introduced on bus speeds and congestion. Such incentives would be intended to encourage Regional Transport Partnerships and/or transport authorities to set targets to improve bus speeds and reduce congestion and to introduce the infrastructure measures necessary to meet such targets.

1.12 Given the central role of partnership in ensuring success in local bus markets, the Action Plan aims to stimulate even greater partnership working between operators and the wider public sector. There is a need for local authorities and Regional Transport Partnerships to work together to ensure that road powers are used effectively for the improvement and promotion of bus services for the benefit of bus passengers and to encourage bus use. Recognising the recent establishment of the Regional Transport Partnerships, the Action Plan aims to make buses an important part of the developing Regional Transport Strategies; it encourages transport authorities to maximise partnership in their areas through the establishment of local bus forums, which will include the general public; and it seeks to ensure that bus planning is integrated into wider planning frameworks, including health and education planning.

Development of the Bus Industry

1.13 The MVA Consultancy report for the Scottish government highlighted the minimum requirements users have of a bus service. Bus services need to deliver a service frequency that meets demand regularly and reliably and which represents value for money, consistently across Scotland.

1.14 The broader concerns raised by the public in correspondence with the Scottish government and MSPs were about the late running of buses, quality of service, personal safety/security, overcrowding and congestion in urban areas.

Partnership Working in Edinburgh and York

Edinburgh aspires to be a city with a transport system that is accessible to all and serves all. It aims to enable short distance journeys to be made without a car and to develop the city to reduce the need for long distance journeys. To achieve this, the Scottish government and the City of Edinburgh Council have made a considerable investment in bus infrastructure and bus passenger priority. Bus passenger priority is provided along essential routes into the city on bus lanes called Greenways. A ring of park and ride sites is being developed round the city serviced by frequent bus services. The main bus station in St Andrews Square was refurbished in 2003, real time information is being rolled out on bus routes across the city, a dedicated Bus Rapid Transit corridor forms part of a bus route and bus passenger priority provided to Edinburgh Airport means it has the highest percentage of bus 'surface access' of any of the UK's major airports.

The city of York is predominantly urban with a historical centre and a population of 180,000. It has produced a Bus Strategy which clearly defines aims, objectives, actions and a timescale for the city working in close partnership through the Quality Bus Partnership of key stakeholders. One of the aims is to make bus travel the preferred mode of transport for all journeys in the city and to prioritise and simplify the routes in the bus network. To support economic growth the main arterial and core routes into the city have been identified to promote the fast and efficient movement of people. This is achieved by deploying bus passenger priority measures, car restraint and infrastructure investment on these routes. Social inclusion is promoted by maintaining a wide network where service may be less frequent or provided by Demand Responsive Transport which then links the less populated areas to the core routes.

1.15 As reflected in The Regional Dimension box, in rural areas the concerns include the availability of services, low frequencies and higher costs. Networks thin out as the population density decreases and passenger numbers decline, making it more difficult for services to pay for themselves and to be frequent. The consequence is, for example, that all bus services are subsidised by deeply rural authorities; and in mixed authorities like Dumfries and Galloway the greatest percentage of services are supported. By contrast, in the four main cities few services are subsidised. Community transport and demand responsive services play a particularly significant role in rural areas.

1.16 In parts of the West of Scotland there are local issues relating to information at bus stops, condition of vehicles, service provision in evenings and on Sundays, poor infrastructure provision such as bus stations and lack of bus passenger priority and traffic control. These concerns are highlighted in the Bus Quality Audits and, particularly regarding service provision, are shared by MSPs.

1.17 Reducing emissions is one of the key strategic outcomes in the National Transport Strategy where the Scottish government is committed to working with Regional Transport Partnerships, local authorities and bus operators to reduce emissions from buses. The review of the Scottish government bus subsidy regime (Action 4 in Chapter 2) will, amongst other things, consider whether a new approach or a more co-ordinated approach is required.

1.18 The seriousness with which we take emission reduction is reflected also in Action 13 to encourage investment in cleaner and more innovative buses. But equally, we anticipate that the overall step change we are seeking in bus service provision will be a considerable benefit not only to individuals and communities but also to the environment through modal shift and increased use of modern, lower emission buses. In line with the National Transport Strategy we will ensure that the impact of Scottish bus policies and the Bus Action Plan are reflected in the proposed carbon balance sheet for transport.

1.19 The Action Plan seeks to develop a more holistic and partnership approach aimed at encouraging modal shift from cars to buses, providing more effective use of current services and integrating land use planning with transport planning. Better integration within planning frameworks will help ensure that the links are made between walking and pathways and the bus network when building new houses or hospitals or shopping centres or schools. More effective planning should help provide the basis for increased use of public transport with a corresponding reduction in congestion which then contributes to improvements in the wider environment. An improvement in the appearance of bus vehicles and the overall experience of using buses could also help achieve a step change.

Effective Implementation of Regulatory Regime

1.20 Bus operators are generally satisfied with the overall regulatory framework but consider that it needs to be applied more vigorously and consistently to drive up quality. This requires the Vehicle and Operator Services Agency to identify and collect information on non-compliance behaviour by operators, targeting areas of concern (as they already increasingly do), and for the Traffic Commissioner to provide enforcement of the current regime. More rigorous enforcement will help address a number of issues such as poor standards of vehicles. Improvements in enforcement are addressed in Actions 15 to 17 in Chapter 2.

The Regional Dimension

West of Scotland

In many areas there are a large number of operators serving particular areas or particular routes in an area. At the same time, there is ample evidence of **poor information** that makes it difficult for passengers, and particularly new passengers, to know when buses actually run and where they go. The Bus Quality Audit noted, for example, that in the Airdrie and Coatbridge areas, only First Glasgow tends to post information at bus stops about its commercial services, and Strathclyde Partnership for Transport (SPT) about its supported services. Moreover, bus stances tend not to have bus flags, making it impossible to know what route numbers are served at the stop.

In Govan, the Audit found that the big operators provided good quality information, but that it was patchier among smaller operators. In Paisley, destination information ranged from good on the vehicles of Arriva and some better smaller operators, to poor and occasionally non-existent on others. Problems with **legal lettering** were found in Airdrie and Coatbridge.

Deficiencies in **bus infrastructure** were found in Paisley, where a number of stops are located at cold and dark spaces under a car park, which many passengers would be wary about using. The Audit also found that, in Renfield and Union Streets in Glasgow, narrow pavements and basic bus shelters provide an unattractive environment for bus passengers.

There are recent examples of developing greater **bus passenger priority** such as Streamline in Glasgow, which provides priority lanes on key corridors and priority at traffic lights in partnership with First Glasgow. But the Audit found little bus passenger priority in Airdrie and Coatbridge. Similarly, in Paisley, there are few bus passenger priorities beyond the central area and buses are delayed in general traffic.

Service provision varies in many areas, though, in the absence of bus stop information, it is difficult to quantify this. The Audit comments, for example, that in Govan service levels drop in the evenings and on Sundays, and that in Cumbernauld – and Paisley – it seems likely that the smaller operators will only provide a Monday to Saturday daytime service.

In terms of the **quality of vehicles**, in Paisley the Audit noted that most of the buses operated by the smaller companies were minibuses or midibuses, with some quite elderly and apparently in poor condition. There was a mix of buses in Airdrie and Coatbridge – some new or low floor buses but also older vehicles that looked or sounded to be in poor condition.

East of Scotland

The predominant feature of the cities in the East is the **high degree of partnership working**.

In Edinburgh, bus transport has benefited from the consistent pro-public transport stance adopted by the City of Edinburgh Council and the extensive network of bus passenger priority Greenways and traffic management in the city centre has attracted extra passengers from cars.

In Aberdeen, a voluntary Quality Partnership for Public Transport was signed by Aberdeen City and Aberdeenshire Councils, First Aberdeen and Stagecoach, refreshed and updated in 2005. The agreement includes a Passenger Charter and over 20 standards and targets that cover all aspects of bus travel.

In Dundee, a Public Transport Partnership Concordat was signed in May 2004 by Dundee City Council, Tayside Police, Strathtay Scottish (now owned by Stagecoach) and Travel Dundee. Under the Concordat, the Council will seek to deliver further bus showcase infrastructure and the bus operators will seek to complement this through a range of measures, including a network review. In September 2005, the Council and Travel Dundee agreed to formalise arrangements through a Best Value Service Level Agreement, Bus Punctuality Improvement Partnership and a Public Transport Information Strategy.

Rural/Small Urban Scotland

The Bus Quality Audit noted that for many people living in market towns the private car is an essential part of life and that car drivers preferred to use their cars because there were no time restraints. There was a recurring theme linked to the **infrequency** – sometimes recognised as inevitable – of buses in less populated areas. The Audit noted further that in rural areas, for people who 'live off the beaten track', there will be bus services for school children with occasional other services to town. Bus journeys would have to be very carefully planned. The Audit commented that, unless something innovative can be done, it seems unlikely that this situation will change.

For deeply rural areas, such as in Angus, the Audit commented that there could be scope to develop something on the **Lincolnshire model**, with minibuses and demand responsive services feeding into the main road services on a regular basis at properly established hubs.

In Dumfries and Galloway, the Audit recorded that there is a strong feeling that the Council is really committed to public transport and is prepared to work in **partnership** with bus operators and the Scottish Executive to raise the quality of bus services. The Council produces seven A5 bus timetable booklets covering its area, including rail times.

EMERGENCY WINDOW
WITH HAMMER

Chapter 2

Aims, Objectives and Actions

Aims, Objectives and Actions

2.1 Taking into account the conclusions reached in Chapter 1, the aims, objectives and actions that follow address the different types of development that are required in different parts of Scotland. They recognise that there is no 'one size fits all' solution, and that all partners need to act in various ways, tailoring solutions to the specific problems that they face.

Effective Transport Planning

To improve bus services through effective transport planning we need:

- a clear vision of how local bus services meet local needs
- greater use of bus plans with explicit actions to deliver vision
- close partnership working between transport authorities and bus operators
- improved communication with all stakeholders.

To achieve these aims and objectives, we will take the following **Actions**.

1. Work with Regional Transport Partnerships to ensure the forthcoming Regional Transport Strategies have a strong bus component.

2. Work with transport authorities to improve bus services, including by establishing Bus Forums in each authority area.

3. Integrate bus planning (including Demand Responsive Transport) with the general, land use, health service and education planning frameworks.

Development of the Bus Industry

To support the development of the bus industry in Scotland we need:

- targeted financial support that meets transport aims (e.g. encouraging investment in cleaner and more innovative buses)
- legislation that supports transport aims
- consideration of national standards where required
- use of Quality Partnerships and Quality Contracts where appropriate
- involvement of all stakeholders
- promotion of accessibility and social inclusion.

To achieve these aims and objectives, we will take the following **Actions**.

4. Review Scottish government funding, with operators and transport authorities, to ensure that it is directed at improving the quality and reliability of services and at enhancing bus infrastructure (e.g. bus passenger priority measures and Bus Rapid Transit).

5. Review Grant Aided Expenditure (GAE) for supported services for its impact on rural areas.

Service Quality Incentive Regime (SQUIRE)

The SQUIRE regime is a service quality and performance incentive regime which is designed to ensure that the rail franchisee (First ScotRail) maintains and improves the services and facilities they provide for rail passengers. There are various criteria including graffiti, litter, seats, staff and customer care.

6. Examine performance-related funding for payment of Bus Service Operators Grant (BSOG), drawing lessons from the Service Quality Incentive Regime (SQUIRE), a rail performance regime; and amend BSOG to allow claims to be made for fully flexible registered services.

7. Expand the Rural Transport Fund.

8. Expand Demand Responsive Transport.

9. In order to support franchising where there is market failure, review the legislation on Quality Contracts (QCs) to simplify the process to be followed by transport authorities.

10. Review the legislation on Quality Partnerships (QPs) to simplify the process and increase the benefits to the passenger.

11. Issue Scotland-specific guidance on Punctuality Improvement Partnerships (PIPs).

12. Liaise with the Department for Transport on enhancements to, and the development of, quality measures.

13. Encourage investment in cleaner and more innovative buses.

14. Working with transport authorities, conduct a nation-wide review of bus stop information.

Effective Implementation of Regulatory Regime

To support effective implementation of the regulatory regime we need:

- public bodies effectively implementing the regulatory regime
- legislation that supports the regulatory regime
- an adequately resourced regime.

To achieve these aims and objectives, we will take the following **Actions**.

15. Establish a protocol with the Traffic Commissioner and the Vehicle and Operator Services Agency (VOSA) to improve the effectiveness of the regulatory regime, including setting time limits for decisions by the Commissioner following a public inquiry, better targeting of inspection by VOSA, and ensuring greater joint working by transport authorities in identifying issues for inspection.

16. Consider legislative changes to the service registration rules to increase the effectiveness of the registration regime.

17. Work with police and local authorities to improve enforcement of bus passenger priorities and no parking at bus stops.

Actions Diagram

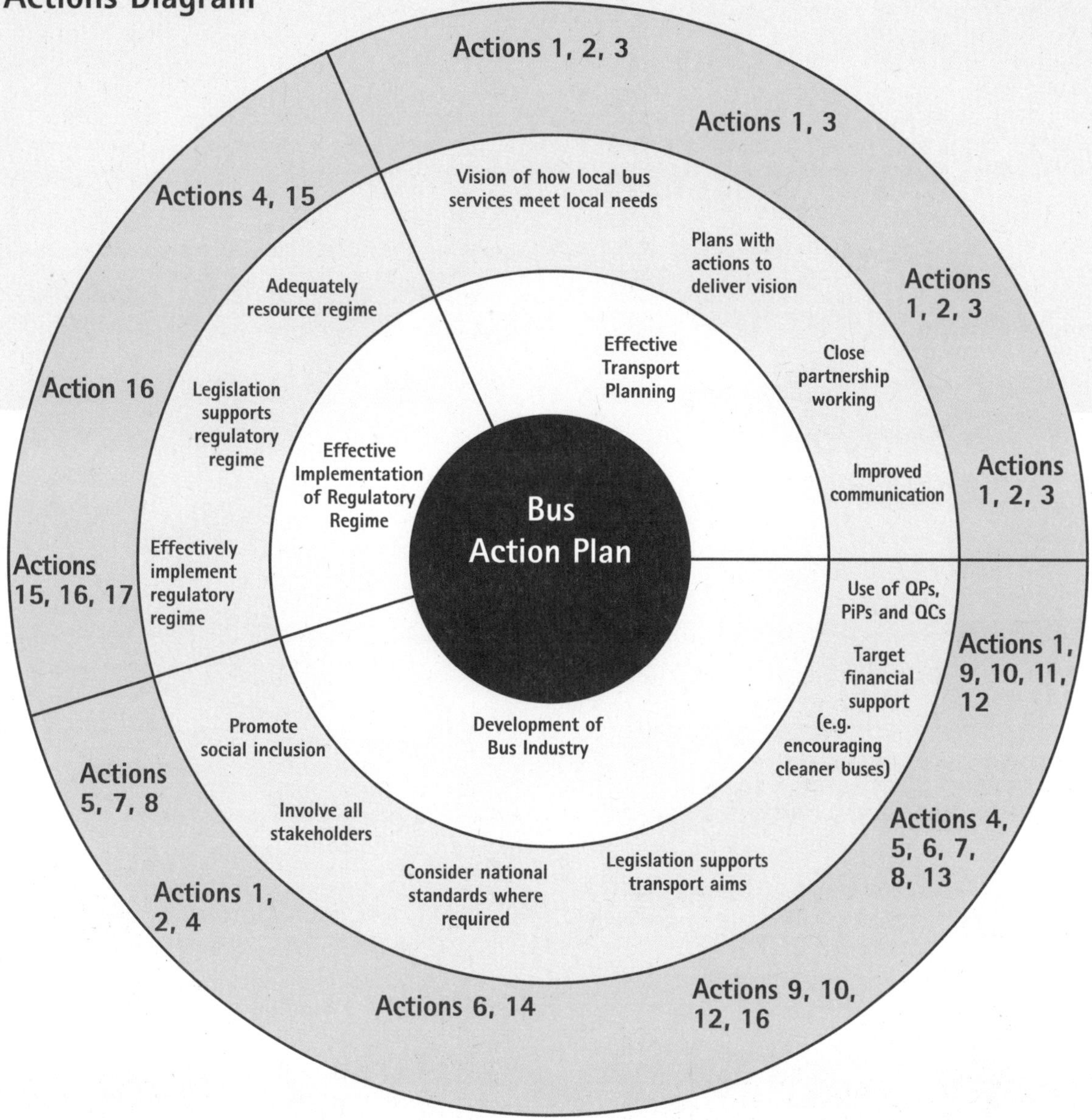

Ashludie Hospital 76
H.3
707
strathtay
ST52 NTO

Chapter 3

Supporting Evidence

3.1 **User Perspective**

The following summarises various concerns which have emerged through material examined for the Bus Policy Overview.

Correspondence on Bus Issues

The Scottish Executive received 112 correspondence cases on bus issues during the period 1 July 2005 to 30 June 2006. The main concern for correspondents was levels of service provision, most notably the withdrawal/reduction of services in Glasgow and its surrounding area. The other issues raised are shown in descending order:

Service reliability
Vehicle quality issues
Stagecoach/Citylink Joint Venture
Bus Route Development Grant
Bus information
Fares
Accessibility
Driver conduct/driving standards
Anti-social behaviour
Regulation/Transport (Scotland) Act 2001

Parliamentary Questions

Sixteen bus policy questions were asked in the period 1 July 2005 to 30 June 2006. Seven of these were from MSPs with constituencies in the SPT area and related mainly to service and subsidy provision and quality improvement measures. The other questions covered Bus Route Development Grant, fares, service provision in the Scottish Borders, and passenger numbers on Perthshire services.

Response from MSPs to Invitation to Comment as Part of the Bus Policy Overview

Fifteen responses were received. Comments were wide ranging including support for better integration and availability of rural transport services, promotion of locally run rural community transport initiatives, enhanced grants, rural fare levels, vehicle accessibility, timetable co-ordination, the impact of service withdrawals (particularly in areas of high deprivation, smaller population centres and where services run at night, provide journey connections or access to NHS services), lack of public consultation on service withdrawals, support for increased regulation to address issues such as 'cherry picking', need for more park and ride facilities and support for driver training in customer care. The Scottish Conservative & Unionist MSPs offered a group response which argued that regulatory interference over bus services should not be increased and that local authorities concerned about their local bus services should examine best practice voluntary partnership working in other areas.

Review of Focus Group Information by MVA Consultancy

Common concerns which emerged were the absence of direct links to key destinations, inadequate bus stop, timetable and travel information, unreliable and poor frequency of services, poor quality of infrastructure and lack of bus passenger priority, personal safety/security while travelling by bus and value for money compared to travel by car. Concerns in the East of Scotland focussed more on frequency of service, lack of direct routes, inadequate information and unreliability compared to concerns about personal safety, lack of bus passenger priority and poor integration between operators (including adverse impacts from competition) in the West of Scotland.

3.2 **Finance for Bus Service Provision**

The Scottish government provided the following finance to bus services in 2005-06: Bus Service Operators Grant of £56.6m; Grant Aided Expenditure for socially necessary services of £26.5m; Bus Route Development Grant funding of £2.5m; Rural Public Passenger Grant funding of £6.1m; Public Transport Fund funding of £18.7m, which has funded, amongst other things, measures to improve personal safety such as well-lit bus stops and CCTV; Regional Transport Partnerships capital funding of £10.5m from 2006-07; and Demand Responsive Transport Scheme allocation of £0.8m.

The concessionary travel Scotland-wide Free Bus Scheme for Older and Disabled People has capped funding of up to £159m in 2006-07. As bus operators are re-imbursed for concessionary travel on the 'no better, no worse' principle, the purpose of the payments received is to compensate for lost passenger revenue and for additional costs arising through taking part in the Scheme.

In addition, there is an £18m investment programme to equip every bus with new ticketing machines and the Young Persons Concessionary Travel Scheme, due to start in January 2007, has a budget of £27-30m each year for discounted travel on public transport.

Bus Service Operators Grant (formerly Fuel Duty Rebate) re-imburses about 80% of the Fuel Duty paid in relation to local registered bus services. The bus industry is the only public transport sector which pays a significant amount of Fuel Duty. Commercial aviation and electric-power rail pay no Fuel Duty. Diesel-powered rail pays a rate of 4.22 pence per litre – compared to bus which pays 47.1 pence per litre gross and 9.42 pence (or 123% more) after receipt of Bus Service Operators Grant.

3.3 Passenger Journeys

Bus passenger numbers in Scotland 1975-2005

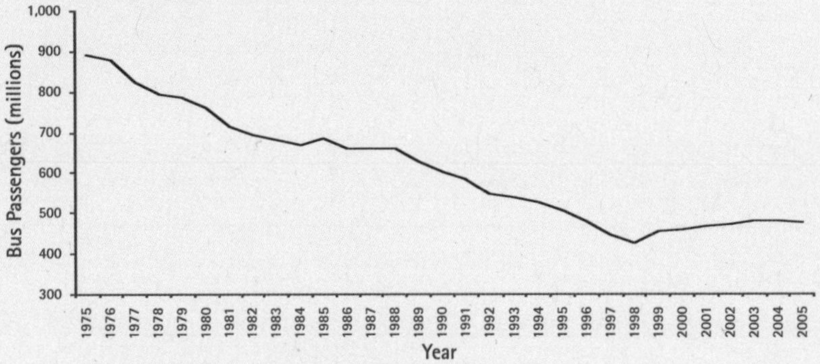

Source: Bus and Coach Statistics: 2004-05
Public Transport Statistics Bulletin GB: 2006 edition

Bus passenger numbers have declined since 1975 but have stabilised in recent years. Recently there has been a **small increase** in bus passenger numbers but this needs to be seen against a background of significant growth in travel concessions since 2002 and substantial falls in bus use from the 1960s and 70s. Key facts are as follows.

- There have been increases in bus passenger journeys in 6 of the last 7 years.
- The number of bus passenger journeys in 2005-06 was 13% above the figure for 1998-99.
- However, of the 479 million passenger journeys in 2004-05, 144.5 million were concessionary journeys. In fact since 2002-03 the number of commercial (i.e. non-concessionary) journeys has been relatively flat.
- The flat trend is still likely to be an improvement over the longer term trend – in terms of total journeys, there were 687 million journeys in 1985-86, 891 million journeys in 1975, and 1,700 million journeys in 1960.

3.4 Regional Variations in Passenger Numbers

Local bus passenger journeys (1994/95=100)

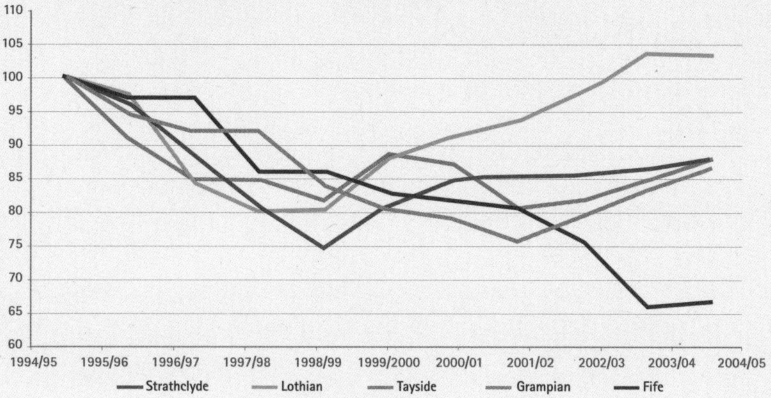

Source: Bus and Coach Statistics 2004-05 - replacement tables

Bus services are delivered locally and the transport plans of local and regional authorities need to address local issues and factors to deliver a bus network that meets local economic and social needs and achieves a step change in performance.

There is a **noticeable variation** in bus use across Scotland. Factors such as rurality, population trends, levels of car ownership and siting of employment centres affect bus use. Between 1998-99 and 2004-05, regional changes in bus use have included:

- no change in Tayside
- an increase of 7% in Strathclyde and Grampian
- an increase of 18% in Lothian.

3.5 **Numbers of Licensed Motor Vehicles**

Licensed motor vehicle numbers in Scotland 1975 - 2004

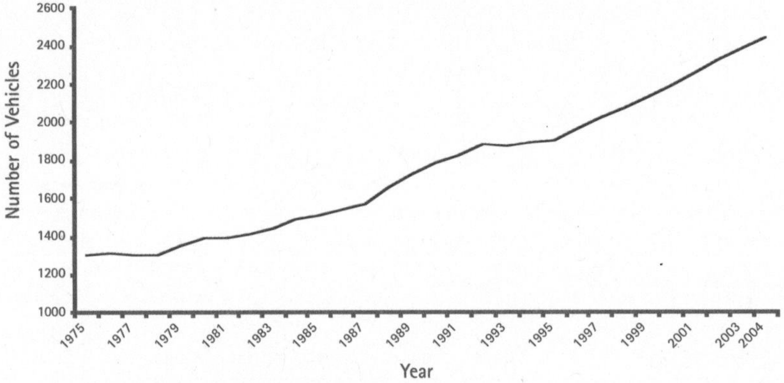

Source: Main Transport Trends - August 2006

Car use has grown substantially over the last 30 years which is a large factor in the reduction in bus passenger journeys. If this trend continues unchanged congestion will increase with a consequential further deterioration of the bus network. To achieve a step change car restraint measures should be considered as part of transport planning.

3.6 Bus Passenger Satisfaction Survey 2005

Satisfaction ratings for overall service and value for money by area

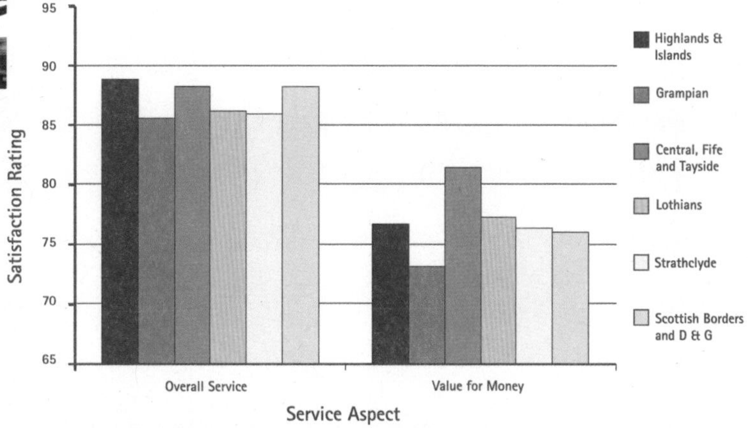

Source: Bus Passenger Satisfaction Survey 2005

The Bus Passenger Satisfaction Survey is an annual survey of some 1,750 people conducted using telephone interviews between 2002-05. The level of satisfaction with 'Overall Service' is at its highest level in 2005. The level of satisfaction with 'Value for Money' is at its lowest level in 2005.

3.7 **Travel to Work by Bus**

Percentage of adults travelling to work by bus

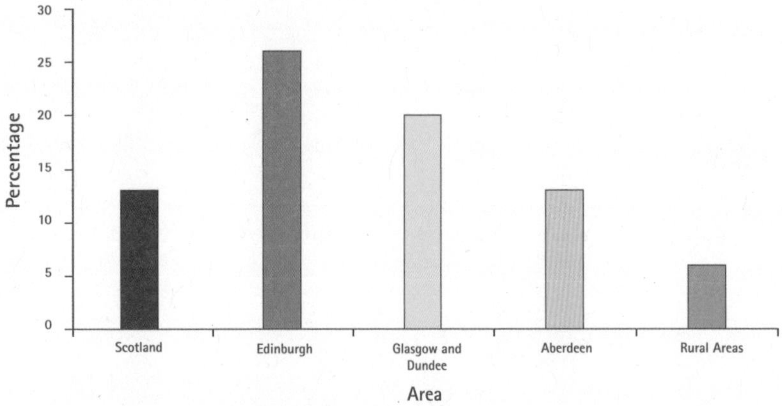

Source: Bus and Coach Statistics: 2004-05

Factors affecting bus use include the availability of a car, service provision, distance travelled, congestion and relative journey times of bus and car. Across Scotland the **percentage of people using the bus for work** is: Scotland - 13%; Edinburgh - 26%; Glasgow and Dundee - 20%; Aberdeen -13%; Rural Areas - 6%.

Individual Operators - Examples of Achievements

First Bus - Glasgow

Entered into a voluntary Quality Partnership with Glasgow City Council; with Glasgow City Council, Strathclyde Partnership for Transport and West Dunbartonshire Council, jointly developed and funded Streamline - an enhanced bus service on key bus corridors; have invested in 220 new low-floor vehicles.

Lothian Buses

A number of achievements, including a simplified bus network and night buses; a flat fare - amongst cheapest in UK; Bus Rapid Transit; close working with local authority developing bus passenger priority; large investment in new vehicles.

Travel Dundee

Achievement of a 100% low-floor bus fleet; establishment of a voluntary Quality Partnership in September 2005 with Dundee City Council, Tayside Police and Stagecoach Fife (Strathtay); Bus Punctuality Improvement Partnership being developed; and a Public Transport Information Strategy to be adopted by 31 December 2006.

3.8 Bus Operators

While there are over 280 bus operators in Scotland, just 6 of the operators provide 93.7% of the bus market. These 6 are shown in the following Chart.

Percentage of Scottish market held by individual operators

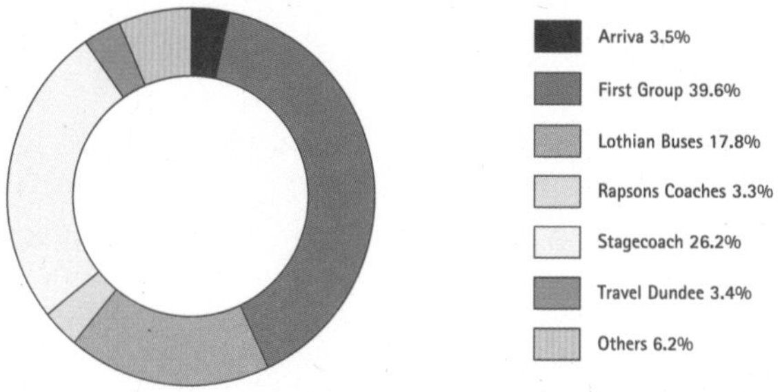

Source: Passenger Transport Monitor Scotland 2006 - TAS UK Passenger Transport Report - Monitoring the UK Public Transport Industry

3.9 Changes since De-regulation in 1986

Change in distance travelled and passenger journeys over time

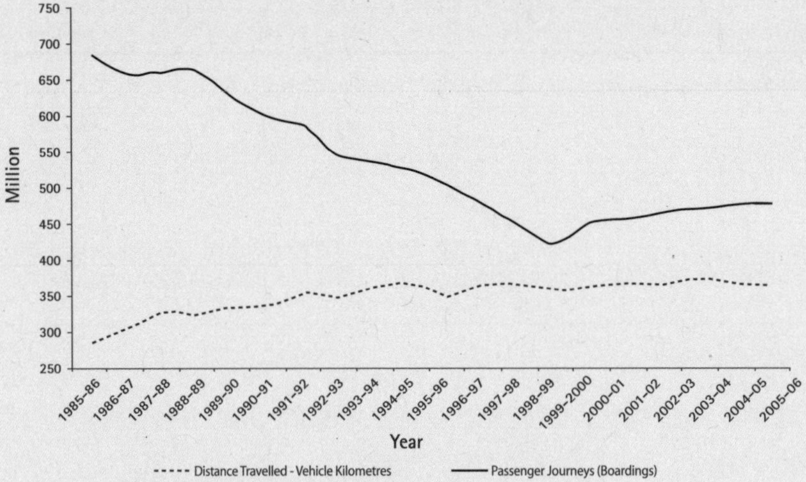

Source: Bus and Coach Statistics: 2004-05
Public Transport Statistics Bulletin GB: 2006 edition

Operating costs at 2004-05 prices

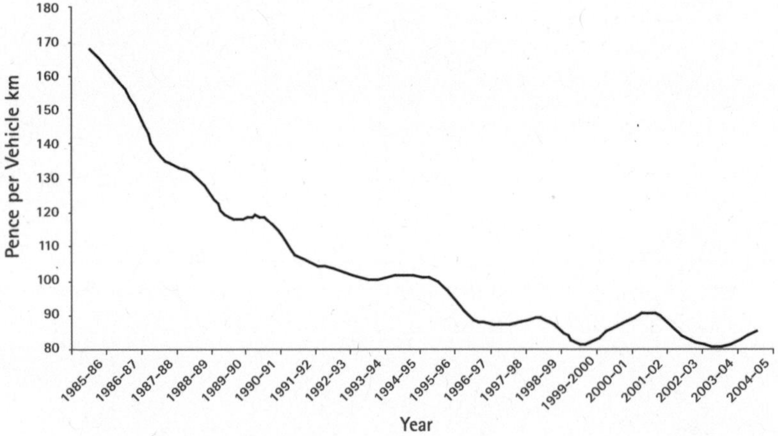

Source: Bus and Coach Statistics: 2004-05

The Transport Act 1985 led to de-regulation of the bus industry and privatisation of most of the bus operators owned by central and local government. Since 1985 passenger numbers have declined, but stabilised over recent years; and the vehicle distance travelled has increased.

There has also been an **increase in the efficiency** of bus operations with substantial reductions in operating costs. But there has also been a **decline in bus use** in comparison to a substantial increase in vehicles licensed, which has resulted in lower passenger receipts. An **increase in distance travelled** has reflected the increased number of buses required to maintain headway due to congestion, the size of the bus network and frequency of operation. In particular, by 2004-05:

- operating costs had been reduced by 49% (in real terms, i.e. after taking account of inflation)
- fares had increased by 19% (in real terms)
- passenger receipts had been reduced by 14% (in real terms) and passenger journeys by 30%
- distance travelled had increased by 28%
- number of motor vehicles licensed had increased by 61%.

Service
Destination
Via
City
Due
F 9 Linwood Y 7
F 62 Baillieston Y 1
F 62 Baillieston Y
Shelter Defect Hotline 0141 810 4610
Glasgow, Argyle Street / Blantyre Street , 6090231
SPT bus
To Linwood
First
2days
BUS STOP MAP
0141 204 0444
Unlimited travel with a ZoneCard from only £12.70 a week.
streamline
the new priority bus system keeping Glasgow moving
As part of the new Streamline service an electronic display providing real-time information has been introduced at this stop. Using the latest technology, GPS tracking and traffic management systems, Streamline will provide a fast, frequent, reliable bus service.
Via